Divorce is Not an Answer

by

Sia F. Dean

authorHOUSE®

AuthorHouse™
1663 Liberty Drive, Suite 200
Bloomington, IN 47403
www.authorhouse.com
Phone: 1-800-839-8640

First published by AuthorHouse 2/28/2008

ISBN: 978-1-4343-5877-6 (sc)
ISBN: 978-1-4343-5878-3 (hc)

Library of Congress Control Number: 2008901920

Printed in the United States of America
Bloomington, Indiana

This book is printed on acid-free paper.

To all the women of this world
The Wife of Noble Character

(Proverbs 31:10-31)

A wife of noble character who can find?
She is worth far more than rubies.

Her husband has full confidence in her
and lacks nothing of value.

She brings him good, not harm,
all the days of her life.

She selects wool and flax
and works with eager hands.

She is like the merchant ships,
bringing her food from afar.

She gets up while it is still dark;
she provides food for her family
and portions for her servant girls.

She considers a field and buys it;
out of her earnings she plants a vineyard.

She sets about her work vigorously;
her arms are strong for her tasks.

She sees that her trading is profitable,
and her lamp does not go out at night.

In her hand she holds the distaff
and grasps the spindle with her fingers.

She opens her arms to the poor
and extends her hands to the needy.

When it snows, she has no fear for her household;
for all of them are clothed in scarlet.

She makes coverings for her bed;
she is clothed in fine linen and purple.

Her husband is respected at the city gate,
where he takes his seat among the elders of the land.

She makes linen garments and sells them,
and supplies the merchants with sashes.

She is clothed with strength and dignity;
she can laugh at the days to come.

She speaks with wisdom,
and faithful instruction is on her tongue.

She watches over the affairs of her household
and does not eat the bread of idleness.

Her children arise and call her blessed;
her husband also, and he praises her:

"Many women do noble things,
but you surpass them all."

Charm is deceptive, and beauty is fleeting;
but a woman who fears the LORD is to be praised.

Give her the reward she has earned,
and let her works bring her praise at the city gate.

TABLE OF CONTENTS

ACKNOWLEDGMENTS

A special thanks to my heavenly father for his faithfulness, goodness, and mercy. He has been good to me.

My thanks go to my husband, Charles S. Dean II, for his loving support and encouragement.

To my pastor, Kofi Noah, who helped with this book — may God bless you.

To my children — Jeneba, Celi, Haja, Ceephas, Jemelle, Charles, and Charlesetta — for their love. You're my treasures.

Much thanks to my father and mother.

To my grandchildren, who make me laugh and make my day.

My Father, My Dad

My eyes seek for flesh
My mind seek for man
Growing up with no father around
The pain, the emptiness that held me down
When I been shoved, where were you to tell me to stand up, stay
strong, hold your head up
Stand your ground
Where were you, not here
No where, never was around

My eyes seek for flesh
My mind seek for man
How will I know how much I am worth to a man
When the one important man had left me feeling worthless.

I am no one's Daddy's little girl
You have left me alone in this world
Mom is not a man
Mom can not replace his space
That fatherly love, touches, his words or embrace

My eyes seek for flesh
My mind seek for man
My hand reached and longed for my dad
That man
Where is he

"Here I am"
that little girl is me

No answer, No hope
I longed
A word came to me

I AM HE ALL THAT YOU NEED!

The father of the fatherless
Not in flesh nor in man
I was the one who was there at your birth
I was the one who held you first
I am the one who gave you life and created your future
Even though you did not know me, I held you when you was
down and loved you unconditionally
That is me
Have faith in me
I am your father
Your Daddy

My eyes no longer seek for flesh
My mind no longer seek for man
My heart is filled
My spirit understands
You are my Father,
You are DAD

Poet: **SREY KONG**

INTRODUCTION

Imagine your confused partner waking you up in the middle of the night to tell you, "I want a divorce. I am tired of this relationship."

The next thing is getting the children together to tell them, "We are sorry, but we are not going to be a family anymore. We are getting a divorce."

Sometimes the children are not told; they just hear the yelling and see the constant fighting.

A cancer has just been diagnosed in the family. Everyone is in shock. Despair and anger start to manifest. It feels like the doctor has just said, "You have three days to live." What are you going to do? The spouse who is not asking for a divorce is in torment, angry and depressed.

The children begin to withdraw. Their attitude starts to change. They don't understand; they become confused, guilty that it's their fault, and sad. The Spirit of Hatred is happy because he has found new victims. These children feel their lives are being ruined because their parents are divorcing.

The other spouse is numbed; doesn't know what to do or how to respond. The world becomes small and the dark cloud of the devil starts to settle.

This is the first symptom of marriage cancer.

This is my husband. Life wasn't fair to him. His parents divorced when he was ten years old. He stayed with his father. Unfortunately, boarding schools became his home. He was moved from boarding school to boarding school because of his shattered world. His behavior became intolerable to people. All because of one bad decision his father made: divorce. It is not an answer.

My husband grew up struggling to keep a relationship. He faced a challenge that seemed nearly inconceivable: Like every human being, he wanted to be loved and accepted, but he didn't know how to give love back and accept the woman he was with. He didn't trust love. Love had failed him once, it would fail him again.

Like every child of divorce, he grew up and never enjoyed the pleasure of a marriage relationship. He had no idea what love felt like or how it felt to love someone. His only experience was the relationship that didn't last between his parents. In his experience, when things didn't work out, he could just walk away from his marriage and ask for a divorce.

He was going around hurting innocent people, and had no idea how to create and maintain a real, good relationship.

Children of divorce are badly frightened that their relationships will fail just like their parents'. My husband's idea was that he would fail in any relationship, so he never committed. He was going around hurting every girl he dated. He would always run when a girl was in love with him, just because he did not know what to give back. He had no regard for women until I met him.

The divorce of his parents haunted him, because of the deceitfulness of the devil from his childhood who told him he would never be in a lasting relationship. This was the reason he had to divorce twice.

Children whose parents divorce are five to ten times more likely to divorce. These are the children who grow up with hate and anger towards the world. The men become rapists, violent towards women, and eventually become homosexuals. The women become prostitutes, thinking that the only way they can pay society back is to have sex with different men. They have no value for sex, so some become lesbians.

They grow up not loving themselves and, in turn, cannot give love. They are bitter inside.

But there is hope. God is a God of second chances. You can fight against this disease, it is not genetic. I was determined to break this cycle in my husband's life. I knew there was something in him that needed to change. I went on my knees and prayed. That's what we are supposed to do; we are not to give up. What happened to your parents cannot happen to you if you are determined to fight against it. Your parents had a bad relationship, but you can change yours to a good one because you are not your parent. You are a different person, if you know who you are and your identity.

In the following pages of this book, I am going to tell you — as the wife of a divorced child who went through two divorces himself — how we can team together to eradicate this cancer that is killing our society today, and leaving our children with broken lives. Fathers make a difference.

Two years into our relationship

LIFE CHALLENGES

I was born and raised in Africa. I was born to Muslim parents. My father is an Alhaji, who went to pilgrimage in Mecca. My mother died at an early age in 1987, shortly after my second child was born. I attended Christian primary school and later went to Muslim secondary school.

Islam was not something new to me. I was learning the Quran for three hours every evening after school. I can even count in Arabic from one to ten. I grew up as a Muslim and later converted to Christianity.

My reason for conversion was that throughout my youth, I struggled, and nothing that I did as a person helped my situation until I had an encounter with Jesus Christ. I used to pray five times a day and fast during Ramadan month, that was part of us. But nothing happened for me as a Muslim. From having my first child, then my second, and what I went through as a woman, my life was adrift. I was married to a Muslim man who had another woman, and who did what he wanted to do without question. I was abused a few times physically; so was the other woman. A few months into the marriage, I started running away from his abuse. Unfortunately, that was not an option, and I would come back. I did that a few times, and the last time I did, that was the end of it. I never returned. So he went and married another woman. I was seven months pregnant with my second child. My father never let me return. My daughter is now twenty years old. Those children grew up with only one parent, and without grandparents. I also grew up seeing my mother struggling to be the best among two other women all married to the same man, my father. Moreover, my father's brother was also married to three women living in the same house. They all lived as though they were all married to the same man — except for my other mother who was living out of town. My father was the one doing the traveling, because she was a professional woman, working outside of the home. I saw rivalry, hatred, jealousy, and betrayal. Life was tough; it became so tough that I knew I had to do something different. It was Christmas Eve in 1984, when my cousin took me to church and I prayed a prayer that came to pass, that I realized that Jesus can answer prayers.

After my breakup, I was on my own. I moved to the city. My next step was to leave the country and travel abroad. With that in my head, I started working on it. One day, I was sitting in the living room when something struck my heart and said to me, "Why don't you go to church?" There was a small church behind my aunt's house. I visited the pastor and he gave me scriptures to read, some prayer verses, and showed me how to fast the Christian way. I did that before I decided that I wanted to travel to America. After doing that, I went to apply for my visa and by the power of

God, and through divine connections, I got my visa to come to America.

When I came to America, I went to live with my cousin in Springfield, Illinois, and later with my boyfriend in Bloomington, Illinois. He had another girlfriend and never told me, but he got rid of her after a couple of weeks and I moved in with him. Life was all right until the same Satan followed me again and disrupted the relationship. I still considered myself a Muslim at that time, even though I had seen the mighty power of Jesus Christ. But nothing was working for me. I was in more trouble. My boyfriend took advantage of me. I was working while he was going to school. I was used and lied to. Coming to America is not easy the first time, because you're naive about the system. People tell you what they think is right, which is not always the truth. When I came, my boyfriend took all my documents from me and kept them for safety, as he said, but later on it became a problem to return. For almost three-and-a-half years, I did not know where my documents were. Every time I asked, we had to fight over it. I remember my first paycheck ever in my life was four-hundred and fifty-six dollars. From that, I was given only twenty dollars as an allowance. Which was okay at the time? This continued for months. Finally, he was finished with school and was working, but things were not all right, and living in a small town you don't always get what you want. One day, we sat and talked about moving to California. He had a friend who lived in San Jose. He got in touch with the friend and agreed that we should move. We moved. We drove thirty-five hours to

California through the mountains and valleys of Colorado and Nevada.

We got to California. Life was going smoothly. I found a job and he had problems finding a job. I was again the breadwinner. For a couple of months, he was having problems finding a job. Finally, he got a job with a temporary agency. With the frustration of not getting a job and the disappointment of moving to a place where things are not going as expected, the pressure was on me. We started having problems. Fighting every time, jealousy kicked in, and every man was my boyfriend. Everyone became his enemy, and the place became small. Again we had to move, this time to Los Angeles. We moved south. This time it was not something we both decided on. So I made him go ahead to find a job, and when he found a job then I would come over. He got a job, and I moved to Los Angeles. When I got to Los Angeles, things were not working at all. We found ourselves fighting a lot, arguing and screaming at each other. All this time, I didn't know where my documents were. One evening, he came home with my documents and kept them in the house. I found them and kept them somewhere different. I knew things were not going to work, and I had something in me telling me to leave. On a Tuesday evening, while he was at work, I packed my stuff and drove thirty-five hours by myself to Springfield, Illinois. I stayed with my cousin for four months and decided to visit my other cousin in Minnesota. I came and liked the city. I went back to Springfield and finally moved to Minnesota. When I moved, I made changes in my life, started going to church, and got baptized. Accepted Jesus Christ into my life.

Today, I say, "Islam is a way of life with no salvation — but the God of Abraham is the way, the truth, and the life with salvation."

I moved to Minnesota in June of 1992, and lived with my cousin. Shortly after, I met my husband. I met him through a friend. I was working with this guy who wanted me, but I didn't want him at all. One morning, he came to work and said he had a friend that he wanted me to meet. I agreed. That afternoon, the friend came to our job at lunchtime. He came to where we were having lunch and sat down at the table. The next thing he did was eat all my lunch, and later left. I was surprised. Two days later, he showed up again. This time, it was not to eat my food, but to look for women. He approached me and asked for my name and number, which I gave to him.

We started dating. Things were perfect. Two weeks later, I was involved in a car accident. I was hurt. He worked night shift and in the morning, he would come and assist me, and drive me to the doctor for treatment. This continued for almost two months, and then we decided to move in together at the beginning of the year. One night before we moved, I called his sister-in-law's house. His ex-girlfriend answered the phone and said, "Your man is lying down in bed with me, you want to come and see?" I for sure wanted to go and see for myself. I took my crutches and left. As I pressed the button for the elevator, it opened and who should I see but him. He asked me where I was going. I told him, and he said to call the house again. I did, and she answered the phone. I handed the phone to him. When he asked her about what she said, she hung up the phone.

In January of 1993, we started living together. The first night, I slept by myself. I though this would be the end. But it was the beginning of a great storm, which I was going to pass through. He had other issues to deal with which I did not know of. The things we did before we moved in together started happening again. Surprisingly, I found out that he had a child by a woman whom he had just separated from. As I confronted him about this, he was furious and became defensive. I couldn't take it anymore, and moved out.

I rented a room in a lady's house and moved out. To my surprise again, the woman he was separated from moved in with her daughter. One morning, I was sleeping when this woman called me and introduced herself to me. I called him and asked him what was she doing there; it ended in an argument and I hung up. I felt bad about myself. I was wondering, why is this happening now? What did I do to deserve this?

He divorced this woman and still lived with her. He said he wanted to help her get on her feet, because their daughter was seven years old and did not have anything to start off with. I agreed because of the child. I knew he was sleeping with this woman and me at the same time. This angered me more, because things weren't exactly how I expected them to be. He spent more time with me to convince me that he was only doing what he was doing for the love of his daughter. With all this going on, I still was crazy about him. And there was nothing I could do at that time, but to pray for

God to keep us together, or to separate us, by his power. And by the power of the Almighty God, we stayed together. Nothing was able to separate us. This is what influenced me to write this book, that divorce is not an answer at all.

WHO ARE YOU?

You see, there is a difference between a man and a woman; we are created differently. Knowing who you are makes it easy to understand your identity. It is like asking for your identity card. Ignorance about your identity can lead you into untold hardship. Ignorance in that regard can lead to one simple mistake that will cost you a divorce. The biggest form of ignorance is for a man to be ignorant of whom he is. People who do not know who they really are, are very dangerous.

"God created man in his own image and likeness. The Father, the Son, and the Holy Spirit". (Genesis 1: 26)

In the beginning, God created the heavens and the earth. And it was beautiful, and then God said, "Let us make man in our own image, in our likeness and let them rule over everything, over the earth, and over all creatures that move along the ground.

So God created man in his own image, in the image of God he created him male. Man was formed from dust of the ground and God breathed into his nostrils the breath of life and man became a living being. Man became a little God, because man was above all creatures of the earth. Man was busy naming all the animals, male and female. There was no one to help him, so God said, "It is not good for the man to be alone. I will make a helper suitable for him." The Lord God caused the man to fall into a deep sleep; and while he was sleeping, he took one of the man's ribs, then the Lord God made a woman from the ribs he had taken out of the man, and he brought her to the man. The man said, "This is now bone of my bone and flesh of my flesh; she shall be called woman, for she was taken out of man."

Man is made in the very image of God. Man is a spirit being and has God-like powers. Man looks like God in some ways, and God looks like man.

Woman is made by God's own hands. And woman was the last of all God's creations.

Man alone received the breath of life, and had been made in God's image and likeness. God made everything beautiful, but his plan was not complete. For the first time, the Creator said something was not good. God knew all along what he would do. He wanted to make a point to the first man and all his descendants who would follow.

God's plan was to add one more creation to the Garden of Eden. A special creation taken from the deep core of man's being, who would bear evidence of God's most delicate creation.

The Lord God said he made a woman. This is different from the way God formed the bodies of man and animals. God took his time to make a woman. He did not put together a mound of dirt to begin his work on woman. He began with the rib of a man. God formed the body of man from the ground, but with woman, God began with the best of man and with his own hands, he rebuilt, remade, hand-crafted, and sculptured a woman. She is a treasure, she is fragile, and she is meant to be handled with gentility, cared for, and cherished for a lifetime. A woman must be treated properly, with all due respect.

God made a woman from the ribs of a man. From the closest thing that God looks at. Why? Because the woman's characteristics are as the ribs — strong, yet delicate and fragile. A woman is to provide protection for the delicate organ in man: his heart. The heart is the center of his being; his lungs hold the breath of life. Woman supports man as the rib cage supports the heart. Man represents God's image, and woman represents God's emotions. You represent God's totality of God. So man, treat woman well, love her, and respect her. In hurting a woman, you hurt God.

WHAT EVERY WOMAN SHOULD KNOW

I was ignorant about who I was and felt unworthy over all that was going on in my life. I realized that I had to find my identity and what I had inside of me. Until women stand up and figure out their identity, they will never know that they were hand-crafted and that they have the power to do anything they want. I believe that what you know, Satan and his agents cannot take from you. Knowing who you are makes a difference. I say to myself every day that I am beautiful, blessed, and destined to prosper.

Let me take this moment and tell you about the hand-craftsmanship of God that is a woman. Put together by the king and her maker.

A woman is one of the most powerful forces in the universe, and that power can be used for good or evil. When God created a woman, he did so with his own hands. He made a woman to build up a man and make him stand taller.

While a woman cannot bring into existence things that are not, she does have the power to build courage into a husband's life, instill confidence in a child's heart, and fan into flames the dying embers of a friend's dreams, draw the lost to Christ, and pray for a better world. That a woman can do.

God created the woman because he knew the man needed somebody. God didn't bother to ask the man's opinion. He just said, "It isn't good for this man to be alone. I am going to make a special helper and assisting partner for him."

First of all, man needs help. Man doesn't know it all, can't do it all, can't have it all — the ability, discernment, and intelligence. Sometimes, man says, "I don't need anybody to help me. After all, I'm a man!" The truth is, every man needs help. Two are better than one.

Women have the insights and abilities that men just don't have. A woman can sense things because God gave her inner radar that is completely accurate. Women function differently. God gave them the inner ability to sense and see what is going on under the surface. They are not impressed with facts and figures; they are too busy scanning the eyes and hearts for fraud and flakiness. Women can see and sense what men may be totally blind to.

Women can smell the bad odor before men do. If there is a skunk hiding under the fast-talker's outfit, they will smell it before men do. Men need to listen to women, because women will save them a lot of grief and some real trouble. God gave women the ability to look past the surface details and straight into the hearts and motives of people. Those are the kinds of abilities women possess when raising children and running a household, and they do pretty well in every other field, too.

Women are better at adapting to changes. God created the woman to adapt to changes, and to help and complete her mate. Women are key agents for change. Women can do a far better job than men when it comes to adjusting to sudden changes, moves, or lifestyle changes. That is because the woman is to be a helpmate to her mate. This is a very special gift from God to a woman.

A woman can bless her man. Any good man of God will tell you that he never realized his full potential until his wife got down on her knees for his life. A godly woman can bless a man as nothing and no one else can. That is because God designed her that way. A godly woman makes her man, home, children, and everything around her better if she wants to, because she is full of power to make things right. She can move mountains, raise valleys, and build a better home. A woman can stop a divorce, make a man jump or dance if she wants to. There is a special thing that a woman has that can make a man's head spin. A woman can make and unmake a man. She has the power to reduce a man to nothing.

God's thought of women is a subject that has engaged the attention of the prophets, poets, and philosophers all through the ages. Unconsciously, to themselves, they are not clear in their minds the divine intent concerning her mission apart from wifehood and motherhood.

God revealed to us his exalted purpose concerning woman when he said: "It is not good that the man should be alone, I will make a helpmate for him and they shall become one flesh," distinct and separate in life, but one. Adam acknowledged her power to lead and did obeisance to her judgments when he followed her in the great transgression.

The world must learn to estimate God's thought of her when he said, "Male and female created he them." God is waiting for the world to recognize his thought of women.

The power of a woman is clearly set forth in history sacred and profane.

Woman, see to it that you use what God has given you, be it in the home, at your job, or wherever. Be faithful to thy trust; hide not thy talent in a matchbox, though it deprives thee of the queenship of home with its subject so sweet and tender. God's thought of a woman is superior to time.

God created woman because there was a serious problem, and he uniquely designed woman to fix it. Surrounded with protection, one who gives assistance in a time of a great danger.

You are important to God and you have strength and beauty all of your own. Ask God to reveal it to you so that you can become the helpmate you were destined to be since the creation of the world. A woman is a crown of creation. The most intricate, amazing, and dazzling creation on earth. She, too, bears the image of God. God wanted to reveal something about him, so he gave us Eve.

What a shame that our race should be this bound, simply because we are not willing to allow God's thought of a woman to enter into the management of the world's affairs and thus make it possible for the kingdom to come, and his love to reign. Let me bring to you some of the women who made history in the Bible, and its account of them. Everywhere the Lord showed up was a woman. Even when he was raised up from the dead, there was a woman there.

The sky is the limit for a woman who walks with the Lord.

Queen Esther fasted and prayed. Lifted up her heart to God, and her hand to the scepter of the king, turned the sword of the foe to his own destruction and saved her people.

God's greatest thought of her seems to have been when he made Mary the mother of redeemed humanity through the incarnate son.

Her power is written in history clearly. Scarcely had the head of Samson rested in the lap of Delilah, when he was shorn of his strength and delivered to his enemies. A woman has the power to do anything she wants to.

Reading the Bible gave me a sense of who I am. It gave me confidence and courage as a WOMAN and filled my inner being. Based on this fact, I came to realize that there is nothing I cannot do, and that I have the power to change my own situation if I don't like it. I will not let society defeat me.

FAMILY ISSUES

This subject is very important to know before you get marry.

"We will remember thy love more" (Song of Solomon 1:1-4). God did not institute family before marriage, God instituted marriage before family; therefore, marriage is superior to family and as a result of the companionship between a man and woman, a family is born. It is very important to be aware of this. And in that context, God respects marriage, which is the nucleus of the family, more than the extended family. Now, marriage is a lifetime relationship between a man and a woman, and is not a five-month relationship or an eight-month one, neither is it a ten-year relationship between a man and a woman. It is a lifetime relationship, which is very important. We don't get into marriage to experiment with it. We don't get a man and experiment whether this man will be good, or get this woman and experiment to see whether she will be my sweet partner. We don't approach marriage with that mentality. So any time you are preparing to work toward or enter into marriage, the first prerequisite is to know that it is a lifetime relationship. When you get in there, you are stuck, no turning back.

There is a reason why God instituted marriage. There are three fundamental purposes for which God instituted this unique union. They are to procreate, to provide companionship, and to be a helpmate. The only thing you have to do is to discover the formula in your marriage. We have several keys that open doors, and there are several formulas that open several marriages; so the formula that will open or lock my marriage is quite different from the formula that will open or lock your marriage. You have to discover and recover your marriage. The first purpose of marriage is to procreate. What I mean by that is, God instituted procreation so that we will give birth and replenish the earth. When a man and woman meet together, an issue has to happen so that the whole earth will be filled with God's people.

The second purpose is companionship. Everybody must satisfy these three requirements in life, and you have to have someone in your life most especially to fulfill this purpose. Loneliness kills. Do not try to be lonely — it kills, it kills your soul and your spirit, that is a fact. You can be with kids, be in the church, be with friends, and even go out to the nightclub, but when all is done and in the night you go in your own bed to lie down alone, you will realize that loneliness kills inside. God knew the consequences of it and said, I am going to institute marriage for companionship. It is very important to know that divorce is not an answer for marriage. You have to keep your wife or husband company, and you have to keep yourself company.

If you go back to creation, you will realize that Adam did not go back and ask God, "Why did you create two of each animal, and you only created me alone?" God himself saw that everything was created two, but he created Adam alone. It was God who said, "I have created everything two, but Adam's helpmate has not been created. I will create somebody who will keep Adam Company. It is not good to be single." When God said that it is not good to be alone, Adam was living in the Garden of Eden with everything in it that was so beautiful; nevertheless, God said it was not good. You can be a multimillionaire and do everything for yourself, but if you are not in a marriage, it is not good. Everyone should have a companion.

Lastly, to be a helpmate (Genesis 2:18-20). We must help each other. God wanted Adam to help Eve, and Eve to help Adam.

Nobody in the world can redefine marriage. Nobody instituted marriage apart from Jehovah himself. God is the only one who has the right to change the formula of marriage, even with the freedom and liberty we have. God wants a man and a woman to marry and stay married forever. God has given us pastors and preachers who are afraid to say the truth about divorce, so it is becoming rampant in our society today. They are compromising the word of God. The time has come to stop diluting the word of God. We must speak it out as it is. Let's get this clear. When we go outside and find a friend or a family member who is getting a divorce, tell them it is against the word of God. Amen!

Now, because marriage is a lifetime commitment, you have to choose wisely. If you don't choose wisely, it will disturb you throughout your life, and that is the background of your marriage. Marry a person of the same clan. Marry someone who you can relate to, and when you speak, the person knows what you are talking about. In choosing wisely, there are some points we have to consider. It is very important to choose the person you want to marry. Be careful and know the sexual life that you are going to choose, because sexual life has a strong effect on a marriage. Check the sexual history and the appetite that both of you have. If you don't check it, then it leads to adultery. There are some men who are very active and need sex all the time, and it is the same for some women. If their sexual needs are not met, they will go outside of the marriage to look for sex. It brings a whole lot of problems into a relationship. It is good to go deep down to check the sexual habits of your spouse. If your spouse is a sex machine and you are weak, then there will be a problem. You will adjust and continue to adjust until you get tired and cannot give in anymore. If both partners are sex machines and can handle each other, then there won't be any problem at all. You must be very careful, or else the partner you choose can either burn you or give you the comfort of your life.

There are five things to check for before getting married. The other person's background is very important to check. Any time you get into a marriage, you are going to build a marital foundation. If that foundation you're going to build upon is destroyed, what can the righteous do? It is very important that you check backgrounds. Check the families they come from, because there are some families you cannot even go near, they stink. There is no good upbringing for the children, when you follow the beauty or love at first sight and go into that family; you are doomed to destruction because the family has no good foundation to stand upon. It is advisable to check sexual life, and go back to check the background of where the person is coming from. For example, my husband grew up in a home where divorce was an answer, and I grew up in home where divorce was never an answer. Check the person's parental background. Is this person coming from a single parent home, or one with both parents home? What are their family values and strengths? This is also very important because who I am determines what my children are going to be. If the person comes from a divorced home, nine times out of ten a person from that background will not be able to hold on to a stable marriage. Those people will always think that divorce is an answer, due to the broken foundation they came from.

If a man or woman comes from a family in which both parents are together, the parents instilled that in their children because it is a good virtue. There are certain things we don't learn in school — faithfulness, honesty. These are virtues that are at the core of life, which we shouldn't neglect. They form a foundation of a character of a man. That puts you to the top. So check the background before getting married, to save you both from the headache.

Motives are also very important. People are sometimes attached to other people because of their body. They need you not for life, but for your good-looking body or good job. Also, because you have plenty of money to support them. People will come around you and exploit you for what you have, and when they have what they need, they will divorce you and go on their way. Some motives are not genuine, so make sure motives are genuine and solidly based on the word of God.

Education is another background that needs to be checked very carefully. A lawyer marrying a secretary with no certificate will always have problems in their home, because their mental understanding is different. While you are speaking of things of substance, your spouse will be speaking about something different, and that brings conflicts or misunderstandings. On the other hand, if both of you are lawyers; you can relate and communicate easily. The parallel ideas sometimes work fine, but it is not good if the sense of reasoning is different. If the two are having diverse reasoning, there will be no good communication in the house. Divorce will be your answer.

AND THE TWO SHALL BECOME ONE

If you know who you are and what you have, you can experience the beauty of marriage, the oneness and faithfulness of God to mankind.

Marriage is a lifetime experience. It is not an experiment. It is the state of being united to a person of the opposite sex as husband or wife, in a consensual and contractual relationship recognized by law. It is also understood to mean that the husband and wife are merging together into a single soul. This is why a man is considered "incomplete" if he is not married, as his soul is only part of a larger whole that remains to be unified.

Marriage is a covenant that exists between God and his people. It is a covenant agreement between two people, sealed with blood. God gave marriage and instituted virginity. It symbolizes the faithfulness of God to mankind. And because marriage is a sacrament, it has lasting value; your promise to each other is until death, to be faithful to each other always. The New Testament compares it to the relationship that exists between Christ and the church. Your fidelity to each other symbolizes and reflects the faithfulness of God to his people, the faithfulness of Christ to his church. God is always faithful to us. If you want to see what God's plan for his people is, you can see it in the fidelity of marriage. Understanding God's purpose for marriage is of the utmost importance, because to marry and miss it is to enter into a life full of frustration and disappointment — setting the stage for great marital unrest. Most of us tend to marry with very romanticized ideas of what marriage is going to be. With great excitement, we anticipate the relationship that will finally meet our romantic and emotional needs. God's primary intention for marriage, however, is not what most of us imagine it to be. He has not designed marriage as a place where we can finally try to have our needs met. He has created it as something much better — something far greater than that. God tends to use marriage to accomplish a very important goal, one that is his primary goal for all Christians. God's primary purpose for marriage is to shape us into the image of his son. If we miss out on this, we are doomed to a life of anxiety and frustration.

Yes, marriage is God's arrangement for lifetime companionship and the arena for our sexual expression, but as with all that he has created, God uses marriage to direct us towards himself. The challenges offered in marriage, he capitalizes on to help shape and mold us into the image of Jesus. We determine our success by how much we are becoming like Christ — loving and honoring our spouse according to the specific roles God has laid out for us in the Scriptures. Far wiser than us, God knows that as we grow into the image of his son our *greatest* needs are met.

Sadly, most of us have been under the false notion that God means for our mate to meet all of our romantic and emotional needs. We marry, fully intending to have our spouse be all that we ever wanted in a mate. Shortly after the wedding, though, we begin to think that our new partner has a lot of changing to do. In fact, it appears they are *far* from being able to fully meet our needs. Instead of being fully committed to *our* idea of what a marriage is all about, they entered in with their *own* ideas of what marriage is to be — along with their own list of needs they expect *us* to meet.

Every marriage relationship tells a story. That's the scary thought, but it's true. Every marriage preaches a sermon! Marriage is intended to be a covenant relationship where promises are made before God and witnesses. Each partner gives promises of fidelity and commitment until death — not divorce — parts them. When these promises have been kept, marriage tells the world about the power of commitment. God uses the picture of marriage as an example of his covenant relationship with his people.

When couples divorce, it spoils the picture. Your marriage is telling a story. What is it saying to the world? It is telling the world that you have failed a challenge and have broken a covenant relationship.

If you have knowledge about marriage and its value, you can make the best out of it. Do not let your marriage tell a story that is not worth telling at all. Its Satan's so-called "deep secret" that only knowledge can reveal to you. Remember that what you know, Satan cannot steal. Divorce is not an answer.

My marriages have stories, too. My first marriage was a bad one. I got married at an early age to a man quite a bit older than I was. I thought getting married to an older rich man was going to make a difference, but it didn't. I had to leave when I was seven months pregnant with my second child. In Africa, where I came from, divorce is not common. I don't even think it exists. A man will just let a woman go. Most marriages are culture-based; the man pays a dowry and that's it, he owns you, and can do whatever he pleases. That means he is free to marry three, even four women, if only he can handle them. And when he dislikes the woman, he will take the woman back to her parents or ask the woman to leave. That will be the end of the marriage. There are no divorce papers, and everything the woman ever worked for stays with the man. No child custody or child support, because the children stay with their father. The woman is left with nothing.

My second marriage, I have been in for fifteen years. This is one marriage I should have checked before I got into. The first six years were a nightmare for me. I went through mental torture. I cried for all those six years. If you come to think of it, marriage is not an easy thing. Just make the best out of it. And I always say, marriage does not bring you happiness.

I married my second husband in March of 1993. We got married in front of a court judge with two witnesses. My ring I bought for myself and his was the ring he married his first wife with. After the wedding, we were supposed to travel to Chicago, but unfortunately, I did not make that trip. He left without me, never told me he was leaving or called me. I call him fifty times, his phone was shut down. When he got back, we had to fight, which did not do me any good. Nothing changed, things kept continuing. Every day was a new thing.

In the summer of 1994, the child and her mother moved out. I moved in. It was a big mistake. One morning, he came to tell me that the child's mother said that I could not be in the house when she was with him, so he was asking that I go spend the weekend with my cousin. I agreed. A month into this arrangement, I thought something wasn't right, so I decided to come to the house on a Saturday night to see if it was true. To my surprise, there was a woman in the house. I tried to open the door with my key. He hid the woman and prevented me from entering, and called the police on me. The policeman came and asked me to leave or he would arrest me. I tried to explain to the policeman, but he wouldn't listen to me. I left and went to my cousin's house. While I was sleeping the next day, a friend of my cousin who was living there tried to rape me. I ran out of the house and called my husband. He told me to come home. That was the end of that story. A week after, I was home when a friend of mine called and said she saw my husband with a woman in the car. That was the same woman who had been in my house. I tried to prove it, and for sure it was true. This was the relationship that really drove me crazy, and I almost lost my man to this other woman. But I was very determined not to lose him. This was the time I was also pregnant with our first child. When I found out, it was in my tubes and I had to do a D&C to get rid of it. I lost the baby. Depressed and frustrated, I was like a time bomb ready to explode at any given time. I felt stupid, because

I was doing everything in the house. He had no money. How could I sit there and let this man to treat me like that?

Life had started to be very disappointing for me. I felt there was nothing to live for. I would drive to the mall and sit in my car and ask myself, why again? What have I done that was so bad that I need to suffer like this? Everything was going through my head. To my surprise, I heard a voice say to me, "Yes, you don't have nothing to live for. Go and kill yourself." I took a gallon of Clorox and drank two cups of it to kill myself. After I drank it, I became nauseated, and I called 911 and his ex-sister-in-law. I was taken to the hospital and was admitted to the psychiatric unit for observation. The ex-sister-in-law called the girlfriend to get his phone number to call him. She called him, but he didn't show up until the next morning. When he did show up, we had an argument. That day, I hated myself for allowing him to treat me like that. My whole world was covered with a dark cloud. No one to turn to; I was alone in isolation. I kept myself out of public view.

Three months later I got pregnant with my son. I went to the doctor for a check-up, and that's when I found out. I had an ultrasound done, but the fetus was not found in my womb, so the doctor told me to come at nine o'clock the next morning for an ultrasound. He said I shouldn't eat anything beforehand. I came home and told my husband; he was so upset and started calling me names. I cried my eyes out until the next morning, praying to my God. That morning I went back to the doctor for the ultrasound, and the baby was in my womb. I came back home, but my husband wasn't there. He did not get home that day until two in the morning.

Throughout the pregnancy, I suffered mentally and physically. I went to the doctor by myself — even when I used to go for fetal monitoring, because the baby's head was pressing on my bladder and I was having lots of pressure and pain. I was by myself at the hospital. I called him to bring me something to eat; he brought me a sandwich with nothing to drink.

I was nine months pregnant when his father and the other daughter came from Africa.

That was April of 1995. His father came to visit, and the daughter came to stay. I felt that it was a divine work of the Almighty God to save my child from the devil's plan. If they had not been there, I could have suffered during childbirth by myself. That was the first time I could smile and sit down to think. From the moment my father-in-law entered our home, things started turning around. My husband and I would sit down and communicate. He would come home on time from work and stay home. Two weeks after they arrived, I had the baby. We had to move to a bigger place because the townhouse we were living in could no longer accommodate us. We moved in June to a three-bedroom townhouse. Things started getting better, but my husband was very uncomfortable because he was afraid of his father. That made him not run the street again. That wasn't his nature. His father became the husband. He was playing the husband role, taking care of our son. He could sense that something was wrong with his son, and that he was pretending. Sooner or later, his true color will be revealed.

My husband started going out again; coming home late and keeping his phone on vibrate. This was also the time he moved his cousin into our home, so I could have people to help with our child. His father did not like what he was doing. My father-in-law decided to have a talk with my husband because of his behavior. When his father confronted him, he lashed out and tried to bring up the past, about his mother. His father never loved his mother, divorcing her for another woman when my husband was ten years old. All the times he visited her, he could see the hurt in her eyes, because his father was his mother's first love. They got married at an early age. From the day of that father-son conversation, things fell apart. We stayed home by ourselves, my husband was never home. We all started going to different churches. Women called the house. It was just us. My father-in-law became my best friend, a husband and a father to me. Everywhere I went, he was there. His daughter also became my responsibility.

Life was still tough. I never gave up. I knew I had to do something to redeem this man who had been haunted by hatred for the world. The father invited his pastor to come over and have a talk with his son and settle some differences. My husband was not in favor of it, but he came anyway. Problems were settled; not all, but some. My husband asked for forgiveness. He was up and down, would stay home for a day or two and go back. Finally, my friend, father, and husband decided to go back to Africa after three years with us. We wanted him to come back to America. Unfortunately, the day he was supposed to leave the country that was the day he passed away. May his soul rest in peace. He will always be remembered.

My marriage was getting better. My husband's cousin was my adviser; I would always complain to him. One day I went to him crying and he sat me down and said to me, "The only thing I can do is to tell you a secret about my cousin. He likes women who can stand up to him. When he has a woman who cannot, he crawls over that woman." I said to myself, thank you for this advice. You will never see me again coming to cry to you. I will stand up for myself from now on. I will leave my job and come home to fight. I became so violent that I was afraid of going to jail.

One night when we were fighting, I took the phone and hit my husband on the head. He needed ten stitches, and I went to jail. All this never helped the situation, it only made it worse. Things were just heading for the worst. I was going crazy thinking that the only way I can stop him is by hurting him to feel my hurt. The more I tried to hurt him, the more I was hurting myself with the pain, too. All this lasted for three months, until I came to my senses that I was only hurting myself. Because no matter what I did, he wasn't paying attention to me. He was just doing his own thing.

My family came to America. Between my marriage and family, life was really bad. They were fourteen people total. I had to get them on their feet. Some had to go to school, and some I had to help to get a job. Alone in the wilderness. Life wasn't fair to me, because there were lots of cultural conflicts and I was the middle person between my family and my husband. There were a lot of conflicts, but they helped my marriage, too, because this made my husband get his act together and slow down. He didn't want my family to know his dirty ways, and what they would think of him in the community, especially my father.

You see, there is a time when storms will come. Stand firm; don't give up. One day at work, I was talking to my co-worker about Jesus Christ when he told me about a pastor who came from Israel and lived with him. I got his number and called him up; he invited me to come over. I went, and we talked about my problems. He explained to me about the devil and how he can steal your marriage and life. All along, I wasn't paying attention to the devil and his tactics. Once we talked, this was the best thing that ever happened to me. There are people who pass through your life, who you have to take seriously. This was a common man who God himself connected me to. I believe in divine connections. God always does something through someone. This man brought a lot of changes in my life. I became very close to him; he became my mentor. One day, he asked me what kind of a job I had. I told him that I worked as a nursing assistant, and he said to me, "You are better than that. God has a purpose for your life, and you have a bright future. Go and do something better." I was in nursing school at that time, but had dropped my classes because of the tension in my life. From that day on, life has not been the same. I immediately called the school and asked if I could register. The school said they had been trying to get a hold of me for a month. The next day, I went and registered for my nursing classes. From that day, I vowed not to quit nursing school. Praise God.

I was thirty-eight years old when I went back to nursing school. With children, a bad marriage, and the stress of school, I was a crazy woman. I was working part-time and going to school full-time. School was hard. I used to leave home at ten a.m. for school, and stay there all day looking for some help before my class started at six p.m. I did this for a good two years. But today, I can sit back and say, "Thank you, Lord," because I had someone to tell me what I needed to hear. Things did not stop there.

The first semester was good; I passed all my classes. The second semester wasn't good. I had problems to deal with. I mean a lot of problems. My husband and I were fighting every day. My family was falling apart because of little arguments, and I wasn't doing well in school. As a result of all this, I ended up failing my classes. You know, God is always faithful to his children. At that time, the school used to have two weeks of class during break to make up the class that you failed, and at the end you could retake the exam. If you passed, then you continued. I took the test and finally passed. I was the happiest woman. Things were very good despite the struggle with day-to-day life. School was going good. I kept on going to school and praying every day not to quit, and for God's strength to carry me. Until the last semester before graduation when things started going bad again when my husband lost his job. With that stress, I failed my last semester. I was short seven points. I had to retake the class.

Let me tell you the goodness of our God. He is a God of lost hope. He will show up when you least expect him to. I had faith. I knew something was going wrong, So I sought Him. I also knew he was the only one who could change every situation. I did not move, because he never slumbered nor slept. I was not happy, but I did not move. All the instructors had to go to a meeting to decide and call people who would take the retake exam. They only allowed students who needed five points or fewer to pass. I was not one of those people. After their meeting, the director called everyone but me. But you know, the spirit was talking to me. Something inside of me was speaking to me, telling me to be still and see the power of God at work. The day of the exam, I showed up to retake the exam. The director allowed me to take the exam, and by God's mighty hand I passed the exam. There is nothing the director could do but let me graduate. I was in shock, even to the day of graduation. After graduation I said to myself, the worst is over — but I lied.

Now came another challenge, the nursing board examination. This is the last exam to get your license to practice. I had to study for it. This took a lot of preparation. I studied for three months, and went to take it. I was so nervous and shaking that I failed it. The exam was too tense for me. I rested for a week. After the rest, I started to pray and fast for three days. This was dry fasting, no food or water for a good three days. I went to God and said, "Father, this test I cannot do by myself, I need your help." I registered for the exam and went to take it. That morning of the exam, I felt the same spirit inside of me telling me to be still again. That's when I knew I was going to pass this time. And a day after my exam, my husband had a dream that I received an envelope with two papers inside of it. That morning, after he told me the dream, I went to the computer and found out that I passed my exam. The third day, the envelope came as my husband had dreamed.

While I was busy with getting back to school, the pastor and I started having Bible studies and prayer in his apartment, but the people at the apartment started complaining about the noise.

So, we moved it to my sister's house. We would meet every Friday evening for Bible study and prayer. I invited him to my house to meet my husband, but you know when the devil is busy, the person can do anything. He came over and my husband attacked him. My husband was very furious and yelling at the pastor. The pastor knew already what was going on, so he did not mind. He asked us to pray. From that moment on, I knew that the devil was really busy with this man I was married to. If he could treat a man of God like that, then he was really a sick man. We started to pray, and while us praying, it was like something came over me. I realized that I had power to completely do something about my marriage, and that I could also do something about my sick husband, because it was not the way things were meant to be. I also realized that God had joined me to all these men because they needed me to come and fight to save their souls. This was a job that God had entrusted me with. It was an assignment given to me by God. I could not run away from it, or say that the grass was greener on the other side, because the grass could be greener sometimes but what about the root? Is it firm or weak; when the storms of life come, will it survive or fall down? That's what a new love is.

Many a time when we marry difficult men, we rush with divorce because we think it is the only way out. No, it is not an answer to a bad marriage. It is not the husband who is difficult; it is the spirit that the devil has put in him that is difficult. It is Satan's so-called "deep secrets." Thank God for a bad marriage, because it's a challenge that you have to always win. God likes challenges.

When you are faced with a challenge, surrender it to God. He will see you through. Remember, you're not alone.

Through it all, I was able to stand in the storm and win. Never give up. Fight to save your marriage. Moreover, fight for your children so that when they grow up, they will not go around hurting innocent people who don't deserve it. Invest in making someone happy, then that person will be able to make you happy. God is looking for people who will fight for righteousness. Embrace life with passion, because it's not the beginning in marriage that matters, it is the way you end your marriage. "Till *death* do us part," NOT divorce.

SATAN'S SO-CALLED "DEEP SECRETS"

This secret that we as human beings need to understand: We need to know that divorce is not an invention of God; it is the invention of Satan. Satan — also called the devil — is a ruler of a kingdom in which he is the god and prince of this world and goes about seeking to devour and enslave men.

His initial appearance in biblical history was with Eve in the Garden of Eden. He is hostile to both man and God. It is his plan to destroy the work of God. He is our adversary.

Out of the raw materials that God created, Satan has built a twisted kingdom that manifests his character. He has an organized intricate agenda and established connections in high places throughout the world, and is successfully moving into positions of authority and control.

He is an evil force, or a symbol of negative energy. He is a powerful spirit being. Even though his mind and heart are twisted with pride, he is highly intelligent, hard-working, and skilled in the art of deception, politics, and diplomacy. A Hitler's ingenious mind and an equally depraved heart

Satan has an insatiable desire to be in sovereign control over every man, woman, and child on this planet. As children of God, we are not to fear him, but we are to take him seriously. He is the enemy of our soul, and will take any opportunity to develop a control base. But equipped with spiritual armor, we will be enabled to be victorious and free.

He gains control by creating and fulfilling needs, creating dependency, and providing the sole source of fulfillment and disaffection. This is the time love feels distant and cold. Unfortunately, disaffection often wins out, and couples who get to the point of divorce never know God's desire for their marriage.

Satan magnifies our weaknesses and fears, and uses them as wedges that come between us. Our minds are his battlefield; that's where he attacks.

Our attitudes define the way we live our lives. They are our emotional feelings. This is what Satan changes first in our marriages, when he builds his cloud over your marriage and brings hell to take it over. The result is called divorce. And he will take as big a bite as he can out of your marriage.

Do not let the evil break your house and make you one of his victims.

Another strategy of the devil is to introduce stress into our lives. We're being pulled in every direction, busy going nowhere fast, having to do more with less time. Before long, tempers flare, hearts break, hurried decisions become bad decisions, and bad decisions make people hurt. Moreover, marriage becomes a perpetual uphill climb, and the hurt makes us irritable, discouraged, and very difficult to live with. That is why we mentally look at and perceive the world, our marriage, and everything around us as bad.

Attitude comes into and affects every area of our lives — our attitude towards our relationship; our attitude towards our family; our attitude towards our business, our job, and our friends.

These are just simple strategies that the devil uses to ruin your marriage. Do not let him win. He is a loser. When Jesus died, he went into the abyss, defeated the devil, and took the victory key from him. All Satan does is to introduce fear into us. He is a defeated fool and powerless.

Satan attacked my marriage by causing lots of argument in my home, which made the house too hostile to live in. We fought all the time, using abusive words, complaining, and throwing things at each other. This really drove my husband away. He had little time to spend at home. He came home from work at eight a.m., took a bath, and left the house, and did not come back home until nine-thirty p.m. When he came home, it was just to get ready for work. This was a routine for months. Friends would call me to tell me they saw him with another woman. Cheating became a part of him. I was so depressed, confused, and frustrated that I wanted to kill myself.

Life was not fun anymore. I started wondering what went wrong, what did I do to deserve this kind of treatment. Was I ugly? These were the questions that ran through my mind. Then I thought about the revelation I received from the Lord, and also remembered reading a little book on prayer at Rainbow Foods. I went and got the book and started reading it. I came across a prayer called "The Golden Key Prayer." It tells you the steps to take when presenting your case to the Lord. As I continued reading the book, I was touched by the fact that it was giving me step-by-step instructions on how to pray and meditate. It also told how to ask God to reveal his will for your life. I asked the Lord to reveal what was going on in my marriage. He said, "The deceiver is out to get you and destroy your life. So you have to stand firm and resist him."

I did exactly what the book said. My faith grew and I developed what I never had — the magic word, "patience." I increased my prayer and fasting life.

Now that Satan's deep secrets — his schemes and strategies to destroy our family, our children, and our life — have been revealed, what are we going to do? Are we going to let him put a hole in our families? Are we going to let Satan and his cohorts tell us that divorce is the easy way out of a bad relationship, or that it's an option? Don't believe him, this liar. This is just to deceive us into making a decision that never brings us happiness, but more trouble and heartache.

Divorce is not an answer for a bad relationship, or when you are married to a difficult man or woman. Let's get together to fight this epidemic that is tiring our families and more so our children. It is a spirit that can be broken with prayer.

DIVORCE

It is not an answer. It is the devil's way of destroying your seeds. There are only two ways of living, a "good way" and a "bad way." The bad way is the way the devil wants us to live. That is, divorce and be miserable. Divorce is a failed challenge, which leads to a broken life. It is a socially transmittable disease that can transfer from one generation to another, and it is spreading fast.

The subject of divorce has been a thorny issue all through the ages. It has been misunderstood by many people. Others have also been made to suffer irreparable damage due to lack of knowledge on the subject. It therefore becomes necessary to have a good and clear understanding of the subject. It can either give you a new lease on life, or it can leave you in ruins for life.

It is the legal separation of a married couple. Normally initiated by one of the parties to the marriage.

There is no single family today who has not either been divorced or has a relative who is divorced. Divorce has actually become so endemic to the society that it cannot continue to be an overlooked subject.

Due to one reason or another, the church of Jesus has woefully failed to touch on or address this subject while there are several of its members who are going through the challenges of divorce, have already been through it, or have relatives who are encountering the problem. To make the situation worse, the church does not know how to relate to divorce. Divorced people are often treated as outcasts or misfits in society.

The church usually takes certain scriptures out of context and ends up making divorce look like the worst sin that can ever be committed. It is therefore necessary to critically delve into the total counsel of the scripture on the subject of divorce, so as to receive proper instruction.

GOD'S IDEA OF DIVORCE

"The Lord hates divorce" (Malachi 2:16) but loves the divorced person, just like he hates sin but loves the sinner.

This is what the devil hangs over our heads: Divorce.

God did not originally plan for divorce in his initial intention for marriage. He did not make any allowance for it.

To God, marriage was to be permanent; divorce was the invention of man.

Divorce in the Old Testament

From the beginning of time, divorce existed, but no mention was made of it until the law given by Moses made a statement concerning it in Deuteronomy. Moses's law on divorce states that a remarried divorced woman who loses her second husband cannot remarry the first husband. To Moses, this is "uncleanness" (Deuteronomy 24:1-3).

In the same law, the word "uncleanness" was given a generic interpretation, which was used to refer to any possible cause of discontent on the part of the man on the basis of which he would divorce his wife.

When you examine the word "uncleanness," the school of thought is that it had to do with sexual immorality.

The Jewish society was male chauvinistic. Men were thought to be superior, and women were regarded as second-class citizens. This meant that men could easily divorce their wives on the slightest issues. For example, if a man did not like his wife's behavior or style of walking, he could divorce her. All he needed to do was to repeat the act three times, say "I cannot marry you again," and at the end of this recitation, he put her away.

Moses's law came in to regulate this practice, which was unfavorable to women. He forbade men from easily disposing of women. The prevalent situation made it easy for the divorced men to remarry, while the women were to remain divorced for the reason of divorce. Moses reassessed the situation. He proposed that, instead of leaving the women unmarried, the men should give the women certificates of divorce to prove that they had been divorced, so they could remarry.

In the Old Testament, divorce was never associated with adultery. Adultery was seen as a capital sin, and an offender had to be stoned to death (Leviticus 20:10, Deuteronomy 22:22).

Divorce in the New Testament

In this portion of the scriptures (Matthew 5:1-23, 27, 31, 19:1-9), Jesus made certain significant statements about sin and divorce: Jesus, in his discourse, made the sins of adultery and divorce equal. Jesus made it clear that God's original plan was that marriage was to be permanent, without divorce. He added that what God put together, let no man put asunder.

He also refuted the traditional punishment for adultery (stoning to death) by equalizing divorce and adultery. By this statement, Jesus was implying that when a man divorces his wife, he commits adultery and must be stoned. In his opinion, the only acceptable precondition for divorce should be adultery or sexual immorality. Jesus made the subject of divorce graver than it was in the Law of Moses. Whereas Moses gave "uncleanness" as the basis for divorce, Jesus used sexual immorality.

Jesus further stressed that a man cannot put his wife away. In the Jewish society, described in the Old Testament, when a master of a slave wanted to put her away, he would get the slave a complete set of clothing and give her some amount of money. However, when it came to marriage, the Jews only prescribed that the woman be given a bill of divorce and sent away. This arrangement did not in any way favor the woman.

Divorce has become a killer in our society today. It is a grave offense against the natural law. The grave sin of divorce infects everybody around it. It wrecks families. Almost half of all marriages end in divorce. Like every major life change, divorce is stressful; it affects the whole family, including the children.

Satan's way of destroying the family from the beginning was to put a break between husband and wife, so he invented divorce and planted it in the minds of people who think it is an option or an easy way out. It is an evil spirit. It is a silent killer of marriage and our children. Its end result is a broken life.

There is a demon out there that's trying to claw and tear your family up — and when he hears of a divorce, he's got a victory.

Divorce is Satan's deep secret; it is the secret to put enmity between husband and wife and wreck their whole generation to come. You see when God exiled Satan from heaven, Satan came to earth and his first target was in the Garden of Eden. It was one of his preferred fields of battle to separate man and woman — one flesh, as God planned it to be.

WHAT CAN YOU DO TO UNVEIL THIS SO-CALLED "DEEP SECRET"?

First of all, you have to know who you are and what you have inside of you. The Bible says, "He that is in me is greater than he that is in the world." (1 John 4: 4) You have to have the Lord in you. You have to accept the Lord Jesus Christ as your Lord and savior.

You see too many couples get married in churches, and it's the first and last day they've ever been in church, just to get married. These are the people who build their marriages on wood, and when hell takes over, their marriages are burned to the ground, their children are wrecked, alcohol becomes their best friend, life becomes meaningless, and the end result is suicide.

More people in our society today are Christmas Christians, who don't embrace Jesus Christ but celebrate his birthday with gifts and Santa. They care more about the holiday gifts, meeting Santa, and the tune of the season. This is inviting Satan into your life.

Remember that you have to know someone to celebrate his birthday.

To unveil Satan's deep secrets, we must first know that he is a liar and that he's the father of all liars. He also goes around looking for someone to destroy. He is a roaring lion looking for prey. So when one confused person, who thinks that divorce is an option or an easy way out of his or her marriage, utters the words "I want out," he takes that and starts lying to you, and starts making you imagine things that are not real. Then you lose the only thing that carries you in life — "patience" for one another.

Patience is the greatest of all virtues; it is the companion of wisdom and the best remedy for everyday life. Relationship is tolerance. You must have patience to tolerate someone. When you show tolerance, then you show love.

Before I continue, let me tell you a little story. My husband was so bad that if women could make men rich, my husband would have been the richest man on this planet Earth. He had women calling from every angle — some he introduced as aunties, some as cousins, and some were his next-door neighbor from Liberia. His eighteen-year-old son came from Liberia and we decided to celebrate his birthday. Two ladies came to the party and he introduced them as his cousins. I was very disturbed and confused, because he had never talked about them being in town. So after the party, I got some information about them and did my investigation. I found out that one of them was his girlfriend; he had been dating this girl for four months. I was so angry that I could punch someone in the face for even coming to my home. But I remembered that patience is the key to everything. What I did was call my friend who was friendly with the girlfriend's friend and made some inquiries.

After I got all the information that I needed, I called the friend up and had some woman-talk with her. When I took him from one girl by praying in the name of Jesus, he would go get another one. This kept on going on until I realized that I had to do something differently. I went to the Bible and read the story of Leah, who wasn't loved. I applied this story to my situation and asked the Lord for help. Genesis 29:31 shows that God has great concern for the wife who is not loved. The Lord sees her misery, hears her cry for help, and will give her a measure of peace and praise. This helped me so much to know that I was not alone. It also gave me something to praise God for.

Unfortunately, many people don't believe that Satan really exists. But he does. Do not underestimate the influence he has. He is powerful, and has brought many good marriages down for lack of knowledge. It does not matter how holy or tongue-speaking, filled with the holy sprit.

Satan is a master deceiver. He is out to mislead us, and to persuade us to believe in something that is not true. He also does that by planting misleading thoughts in our minds.

He entices us to do things that are contrary to the will of God. He is a tempter who tempts us to sin. He will come at us with every weapon he has. He doesn't care who we are or how much power and influence we have. He goes after every man, woman, and child. We are his enemies, and he is after our souls. He will not stop until Jesus comes again. You must know that he is after us. We must be prepared, be alert, and recognize when we are under attack.

The one weapon we have to wage war against his deep secret comes from God. It is only ours by virtue of our relationship with God; without him, we are truly nothing. You must accept the man named Jesus Christ in your life.

Brothers and sisters, let's stop Satan from destroying our lives. He has done more harm to our dying world. Divorce has taken a huge toll in our society today. Don't let one mistake cause you a broken life.

WHAT CAN YOU DO TO PUT SATAN'S DEEP SECRETS IN REVERSE

Do you feel you are at a dead end in your marriage? Is your spouse threatening divorce? What can you do to change your circumstances? Is your spouse involved with another person? What could you do to break up that relationship? What can you do to change your spouse's hardened heart?

Cry out to the Lord and ask him to help with your marriage. He holds the heart of man, he can change it if you ask him to.

The answer to every one of the questions above is to use the spiritual weapon that God has given us by praying for your spouse. The reason you want to pray is to break the chains of wickedness, to undo or loose the chains of the bondage of sin, for your spouse or loved one to be set free. Your spouse may be tied up or a captive to sin, adultery, anger, abuse, or pride, to name just a few. There is power in prayer, and a remarkable result can be accomplished in the lives of others.

I know most women do not want to hear this; more women file for divorce than men, because the law favors us. Moreover, we think it's a way of getting our life back. God has given women the power to change this dilemma. He has given us power to overcome circumstances. I think that a woman has more to lose in a divorce than a man. Think about the children, all that you have invested in the marriage. A woman needs to stand firm and build her root, protect her man, fight for her children, and resist that spirit of divorce. Every wife holds her marriage; do not let anyone snatch your man from you and make your children live in a fatherless home by filing for divorce. If you can train a dog, you can tame a man. Men are very weak. There is something special about a woman. There is nothing like a praying mother, or wife. God hears our prayers.

As I said before, God created one man and formed one woman; through this woman, generations have come. Why doesn't every woman look back and see that the world is full of her seed, and that it is her seed that Satan wants to destroy? Satan did not go to Adam, because he knew that once Eve is weakening, Adam will be easy to destroy. This is the same way with our marriages; when there is disaffection in women, it weakens women, which gives Satan the power to introduce the spirit of lust in men, telling them to look outside for affection, which results in fornication and adultery. This is the start of an attack on your marriage.

I was married to a man outside of my clan, difficult to be with and an unbeliever who went to church on Sundays at noon, and walked right back out if he did not like the preaching for that Sunday. He used to go to church to let people see him. He did not like to read the Bible, and if he went to church and liked the preaching, he interpreted it in his own words to suit himself. There are complications in marrying out of your clan. My husband is a Liberian and a Christian; I am a Sierra Leonean with a Muslim background. If you are a believer, you need to marry someone who believes as you do! I realized he just did not respect any women, and that he had an issue with women. He was in bondage. He argued a lot, screamed, cursed, and was full of anger. He liked to hang out with friends, go to nightclubs, and party a lot. He had women all around, and when I brought him to the Lord in prayer, he would go finding another one. He was full of lust. I used to sit down and cry all day by myself, wondering what mess I had gotten myself into. The more he tortured me, the more I found myself loving him. He was not a father to his children, he was always gone. I am an introvert who likes to stay home and enjoy the beauty of the home. Where I came from, women were supposed to be in the house at all times. As a Muslim woman at that time, growing up was tough. We were restricted in certain ways, wherein some things we did and some we were not allowed to do — like not wearing pants, covering our head, speak when asked, and not sitting where men were sitting. This life was very difficult to live. My husband was complaining all the time because I was boring. I was very miserable in my relationship.

For six years, this nonsense continued, until I discovered that fasting was what I needed to add to my prayer life. It is a very important spiritual weapon if you want spiritual breakthrough in your marriage. I pray that you will start to fast for your spouse and your children to be set free from the slavery of sin that they are living in.

The first purpose of fasting is to draw you closer to your Lord God. The weapon of prayer and fasting has been known to do wonder when other methods have failed. In addition, you need to ask your Lord to cleanse your own heart of any and all impurities, so you will be acceptable to God.

I felt that my husband was headed straight towards hell, and I did not know what else to do. I had a choice to leave him, but I was not ready to give Satan the satisfaction of breaking my marriage. I feared God's justice as well as knowing his mercy and grace. I also felt that it was my duty to save a soul from the world of wickedness and from the bondage of Satan.

The truth was that, in spite of all that my husband had been doing to me, I still loved him very much. Our children needed their father, and I needed my husband. And I finally realized that, as my Lord revealed to me, our problems were due to the enemy, Satan, coming to steal, kill, and destroy our marriage and family. I felt I had to fight back with as much power as the Lord taught me in his words. I then fasted for myself, my husband, and the children.

You see, the Lord sees our misery, hears our cry for help, and will give us a measure of peace and praise. Prayer will help make a bad marriage better without hurting or using people. God has a great concern for the wife who is in a messy relationship.

With all this knowledge and truth, I knew I had to fight to bring back my man from the captivity and the slavery of sin. Fasting was a routine for me. Every prayer group I heard about I would join. I cut negative people off and only concentrated on my problems and my children. We have seven children total. They all needed their father. They had a dad, but not a father. I could feel their pain and see their frustration. First, I had to pray for myself before I could pray for them.

I prayed for God to numb me, and asked him that, if this was the right man for me, to please make the relationship work. If not, to give me the courage to walk away. The more I prayed this prayer, the more I got hope and courage to stay.

I also prayed for quietness. To keep quiet and it worked. Through my own marriage, I discovered that patience meant biting my tongue when I felt like wagging it. It meant learning to shut up and pray. When I did open my mouth to vent, something would hold my mouth. For three years, I thought about telling my husband my every thought —thinking it was "constructive communication." It was destructive instead, because my husband wasn't interested whatsoever in what I had to say. When I realized that, things started to improve. There was a point at which I had to agree to whatever he had to say, because I knew arguing would not help the situation, it would cause more problems. Arguing in a marriage is very destructive. It creates more trouble, and frightens the children.

If there is one thing you can do, it is to stand strongly by your family and say to Satan, "I am not going to let you tear my family apart. I know your secrets, and I am not going to let my children suffer because of your lies. I am going to hit you with all I have 'in the name of Jesus.'" Satan needs to be stopped, and until all women stand up and unveil his ugly tactics, he will not stop. Our husbands, sons, and brothers will always be his victims. His aim is to destroy the innocent. Divorce is not an option; you need to know that very deeply. It brings us more sorrow than happiness. It destroys our children, who don't deserve the mental torture. Taking children from the only home they know and from the other parent is scattering their life. Don't hand your child the key to hell through divorce; hand them the key to heaven with prayer

I have heard some people ask how I could stay in a relationship because of the children. Well let me tell you something. You are not staying in it because of the children. You are staying because you are about to save a dying soul. Someone who needs deliverance from the hands of Satan, and that person is you. When a man and woman are married, they become one. They are no longer two. If you cannot pray for your husband to be saved, how then can you pray for your son to have happiness? We worry more about some things that don't bring us happiness in life. And the things that bring us happiness, blessing, and salvation we do not worry about. Think about the nine months you suffered to bring an innocent person into this world. Is that person not worth fighting for?

Society still holds women responsible for the family, whether in a married family or a divorced one. Women have a sole responsibility to carry the family.

Another one of Satan's so-called deep secrets that needs to be unveiled is adultery. We all can be hurt by this act, but should this give us grounds for divorce? Adultery is not a mandatory reason for a divorce. If it were, that would mean that we could, according to Jesus, divorce our spouse if he only committed the act of adultery in his heart. This is a spirit that is introduced into your marriage, and it hinders most marriages today. This is one of Satan's most dangerous deep secrets that affect most people in life. Not satisfied with one woman or man. It is so destructive, because it strikes at the very heart of God's gift of marriage; it takes the human bond of trust and intimacy and the God-given bond of spiritual unity, and shatters them both. Adultery is only a symptom of a greater problem within a framework of the marriage. It is the legal "gotcha," but I don't think it causes divorces; it's a symptom. It is very difficult to know that you are sharing your man or woman with another person. How many will admit that they have not fornicated? This is a sin, but who are we to judge one another? Why will you leave a person for adultery, allowing the person he or she cheated with to win while you suffer mental torment or destroy your own life because you hate the idea. It is truly a sin, but are we to divorce a person who is being controlled by a spirit or dying from sin? Where is the forgiveness and mercy? Jesus showed mercy to the woman who was caught in adultery, even though there were consequences. Why? He wants us to forgive one another. Consider your spouse as a sick person dying from a spirit of adultery, someone who needs you. Remember that if any one of us becomes a Christian, then God has already forgiven us from the sin of adultery. Therefore, it is not our place to condemn and judge others caught in sexual sin. And more so, it is not our place to withhold forgiveness from others for anything they've done against us. There is forgiveness for sexual sin. This is not a license for divorce; the person is sick and desperately needs your help to break this habit. Adultery is in the head and not the heart. It plays in the head and disassociates itself from the heart. We shouldn't give them divorce as their medicine, but pray for them and ask God to heal them because divorce is not an answer.

TO EVERY CAUSE, THERE IS AN EFFECT.

No couple goes into marriage thinking they will be the ones who won't make it. If we make it till death do us part, we have made God happy. But if we fail through divorce, there are consequences that we must suffer.

The only legacy a divorce leaves behind is a broken heart. When we are joined to another person, an emotional attachment or bond is formed. The souls of the two persons are united. Each of them begins to depend on the other for solace and comfort; they have a spiritual, emotional, and physical tie. As a result, no one has ever gone through a divorce unscathed.

All who go through a divorce come out with pain, and have to cope with great distress and traumatic experience. Their souls are torn apart. They go through various challenges.

The children are sometimes left open to demonic harassment, fear, and all kinds of negative pressures and reactions. Some children are known to have nightmares, others have their grades fall at school, and others begin to experience emotional disturbances.

For the partners involved, recovery is a difficult and painful process. It is a known fact that 80 percent of all female mental cases are due to divorces and a broken heart. A deep hole remains in their hearts and hatred builds up; whoever their spouses are with becomes the target. Their self-esteem is shattered, and it influences their ability to be a positive role model. The men are tortured emotionally with all kinds of restrictions. As a result of their parents' pain, the children involved suffer also, because of one confused person who thought that divorce was an answer to the problem. This is a grave decision that we need to rethink.

There is no marriage without problems and conflicts. Many assume that Christians do not have conflicts in their marriages or relationships. With this wrong notion, many are surprised and hurt by the conflicts they find in their marriages. As a result, some are led to fall out of their relationship and have their marriage dissolved. Marital relationships were intended by God to be permanent, hence couples must be aware that they are bound to have conflicts and therefore must learn how to handle, deal, and cope with their partners. No matter the type of spouse one finds, he or she must learn to live harmoniously with the partner. Divorce is not an answer; it can be detrimental to a person's well-being.

One of the basic causes of conflict in relationships is the lack of understanding of the temperament of our spouse. The Greek scholar Hippocrates wrote that there are four different temperaments that are results of the kind of fluid that flows through a person's body that, if not treated, can lead to conflicts, hence divorce:

Sanguine: These are people who are warm-blooded.

Choleric: They have yellow bile flowing through them.

Melancholic: These are those with dark blood flowing through them.

Phlegmatic: They have phlegm or mucous circulating in their system.

All these temperaments have their strengths and weaknesses. Therefore, there is a need for every partner to know and learn how to live with the other party's temperament to enable them to have a successful relationship. Failure to understand each other may lead to conflicts, separation, divorce, and later consequences.

Let's look at the characteristics of the different temperaments.

SANGUINE

Strengths: People with this temperament are warm-hearted, spontaneous, enthusiastic, sociable, lively, and free-mixers. They can do things impulsively; have much zeal and passion for whatever they want to do; and make friends easily. They also enjoy many friends. The Sanguine husband may invite his friends home without first obtaining permission or counsel from his wife. He expresses his emotions easily. When he is happy, he will talk continuously. In the same way, when he is offended, he will make you aware of it immediately.

Weaknesses: They are impulsive, talkative, and weak-willed; they compromise easily, and their moods change rapidly. They are found to be happy one minute and sad the next. They love to have the attention of everyone. Sanguine people usually make many promises that they often fail to honor because there are so many. This is very peculiar to Sanguine people who have not been transformed by the power of God. A Sanguine husband can easily spend his salary on items he did not budget for, and he will have given out most of these things to his friends before reaching home. Similarly, the Sanguine wife would also buy many items she did not initially intend to buy on her shopping trip.

CHOLERIC

Strengths: People with this temperament are confident, pioneering, and adventurous. They like to do things no one else has done. They are also purposeful, strong-willed, decisive, and self-disciplined — natural leaders and organizers.

Weaknesses: They are emotionally deficient — they will make their point in spite of the other person's tears. They are unsympathetic, domineering, impatient, and do not want others to glory in their achievements and successes. The Choleric partner will always argue out his points clearly. He is always logical and organized in his thoughts. The Choleric partner always comes out as the natural leader in every situation. However, he is so self-sufficient. He would also win in any argument because, even when he is making a mistake, he does it with conviction. He does the wrong thing with the same might and purpose he would do the right. Moreover, when he becomes convinced of a wrong, he can easily make a complete turnaround with equal zeal and purpose to get things corrected. The Choleric partner would always get you wondering at the difference between his pronouncements and actions. He can change his course anytime.

MELANCHOLIC

Strengths: People with this temperament are very analytical, highly gifted, creative, self-sacrificing, and loyal. They prefer to avoid the limelight and like to maintain high standards.

Weaknesses: They are introspective — always thinking within and on the inside. Their thoughts are not loud, but they are very critical, very touchy, very moody, sensitive, and excessively analytical. They will always read between the lines, are very suspicious of all things and of all persons. They are also very calculating, easily annoyed, very pessimistic, and will always discourage new ventures. They are indecisive, but are perfectionists who insist on the minute details and always put themselves down. The Melancholic wife would not even allow her husband to move a glass to a position different from where she placed it. She would not take kindly to you and your friends messing up her well-swept home. The Melancholic husband expects his meal to be made at a special time, and will not accept any delays. He will insist on the ingredients to be used to make the meal and the method to be used.

PHLEGMATIC

Strengths: People with this temperament are calm, easygoing, faithful, reliable, and can control their emotions. They are peacemakers, always think before acting, and have a high sense of tolerance. They also have a dry sense of humor and love to create fun that could be expensive at times.

Weaknesses: They lack energy and are indecisive, fearful, self-centered, and reluctant to become involved. They are also unenthusiastic, unresponsive, sarcastic, and lack initiative. The Phlegmatic husband would leave all the decision-making to his wife, even in matters of how the money would be spent, and how the children should be raised. The Phlegmatic wife would also leave the decision-making to her husband. She would not be involved, neither would she complain.

None of these temperaments is better than the others. Unfortunately, many times, the conflicts in the home are brought on by one partner's desire to change the other. It must be noted that a person can change when these factors are present.

But you have to want to change, know what to change to, and have encouragement to change. Spouses must learn to cope with and not try to deal with their partners. It is God himself who created these temperaments. Hence, each partner must learn to live with the other. This will help to reduce divorce rates in our society.

WE CAN DO IT

I don't care if you've heard the words "I'm not in love with you anymore," or "I don't feel the same way about you," or "I need my space." I am telling you that feelings can change, and marriages can be revived and restored.

We can do it with the help of God. Jesus is Lord. Do not look to fix your marriage. It is not an experiment, it is a challenge. You cannot fix a challenge by taking trips or going for counseling. Many times, I hear people say they went for counseling and it failed. It failed because marriage counselors don't hold the heart of a man. Besides, they make things worse. For example, when I took my husband to a marriage counselor to try and fix our marriage, I was told to leave him because he was the worst man to be married to. Marriage is not a test, it is a covenant, and only God can revive and restore it. When you are faced with a challenge, lean on the everlasting arm. In marriage, you have to win. I was very much determined to win. I failed the first time, so I vowed not to lose the second time. During my trials, I had a revelation that God created me to be a powerful woman who can change my world and my marriage for the good, and that there is nothing I cannot do. This revelation put me on a cause to discover and pursue my purpose. I also found that my pain will help me pursue my purpose. So I sought the Lord with prayer and three days of dry fasting (no water or food). When you are desperate, you do desperate things. I knew I had the power to change my situation, because the future of my marriage rested in my hands. I asked the Lord to forgive me for all the times I had failed him by trying to do things my way — that is, the arguments, yelling, fighting, and cursing. This is very important to do if you want healing in your marriage. Then I asked God again to help me find it easy to forgive my husband for all the hurt and what he put me through. If you don't forgive, God will not forgive you. The more I prayed this prayer, the easier it became to forgive him. Then I asked for strength to go into Satan's camp to take what belongs to me — my husband. This is the hardest part, because you have to know that you are not fighting against flesh and blood, but principalities and powers of darkness. It wasn't easy, but I was going to do everything in my power to have him any way. I knew God holds the heart of man, and has the power to revive him. Call upon God, and he will answer you. He answered me when I call on him. No matter what your situation is or what you are going through, divorce is not an answer. It is Satan's way of destroying us. Call on the Lord.

Years later, I noticed my husband coming around. One Sunday morning, I was getting ready for church when I heard him say, "I am going with you to your church." I went into my closet and praised my God for his goodness. He is faithful because he never fails. We were created for times like this. I believed that God is who he said he is.

God is depending on every woman on this earth to restore his children. This is our sole responsibility to this world. But we have gone outside of our role to fight for equality, instead of praying for our children. The prisons are full of our children, the streets are also packed with our children stealing, raping, and causing all kinds of crimes. Our families are in trouble, our marriages are in trouble. Where are all the women? What are we doing? Each of us will come to a point in life when we realize we must change our situation. These moments are painful and intense. But take heart; you are not alone. I strongly believe in the power of a woman. I want every woman to realize her power and begin to use it positively to change her marriage and her husband. You have more power over your partner. Do not let any man fool you. God has given us all his power to make our marriages work.

Our society is severely in need of positive, powerful women, and I believe that you are one of those women, who have the power to open the eye of the blind. Divorce is a spirit; these spirits and evil forces can be commanded.

Because we possess the power, we don't have to sit by and let divorce ruin our families; we can do something about it. There is an epidemic in our society of hopelessness and helplessness that needs to be dealt with.

I tell you the truth, marriage is tough! But divorce is killing. Tough situations never last, but tough people last. There are disagreements and other things, but the ability to accept, forgive, and love must be honored and cherished every day. You need to honor your spouse. You need to respect his position in the marriage and you desperately need to stop analyzing, reviewing, and basing your marriage on your spouse's faults and weakness. Be aware that with God's guidance, you can learn to humble your proud and selfish ego. You will see beyond the weakness of your spouse and forgive him with the loving kindness that, if he is remorseful for his actions, he deserves from you as his spouse. Also stop pressuring, criticizing, complaining, and most of all stop whining about everything. Remember that nobody wants to be married to someone holding a gun over his head. Please get rid of hostility and supporting negativism, and agree with anything your spouse says or does. Put a good name on it.

A marriage is only as strong as its foundation. The groundwork for our lives is adopting the spirit of Jesus Christ; he is the support, which holds up the marriage when under pressure.

Your marriage won't be back right away, but by showing each other the willingness to trust God, and putting him first in your own life, you will show your spouse what your true intentions are for the marriage.

We can revive our dead marriages. It's worth a try. Divorce is not an answer, it just adds up to more gays and lesbians. We are to stop this evil corruption in our society. Let's don't give Satan charge over our lives, our marriages, and our children. It's our real seed that suffers; it's your children who will suffer because of one mistake you make, by divorce. Don't give up.

Brothers and sisters, Satan is stupid. I was so mad at his deceitful lies that one day I said enough is enough; I will not let Satan win over me. I stopped worrying about my problems and concentrated on Jesus. We need to confront some things in life and deal with them once and for all.

Divorce is something we must deal with, and whatever comes with it! We are not to play around with it, because its end result is destruction. Another thing we get confused about is LOVE and FEELINGS. Love is not feeling first. Love begins with a desire to please God. Love towards another is a willingness to give him whatever you have that he needs, because you know that God wants you to. Where true love exists, the feeling follows soon enough. Love is first manifested through giving. Feeling is self-centered; love focuses upon another. Love is tied to giving, never to feeling. That is, therefore, where you must begin; you must learn to give love. You must give to one another all that you have that the other needs. It will not always be easy, since you have developed patterns of wanting and expecting and demanding rather than patterns of giving. All of that will have to change. And you will have to learn to give love even when the other party is not very loving or lovable towards you. Never stop loving.

Forgiveness is not feeling first either. It is fundamentally a promise. When you put your faith in Christ as your savior, God promised to never remember your sins against you anymore. When you forgive one another, therefore, you are promising to do three things toward his wrongdoings: You promise not to use them against your spouse in the future, not to talk to others about them, and finally, not to dwell on them yourself.

There are also responsibilities pertaining to marriage. The man is the head of his home, as Christ is the head of the Church. That means that he is primarily responsible for seeing to it that there is love in the home. Headship has its authority, but we shall begin with its responsibilities. To take living leadership in the home, a man must follow the models provided by Christ in his loving headship over his Church. If there is no love in the house, it is the man's fault. That man has failed not only his wife but his manly responsibilities. Now, the wife. God does not require love of the wife as the essence of her role in the home. He does insist upon submission: As the Church is subject to Christ, so let wives also be subject to their husbands, that is, pray for your husband, your children, and yourself. Remember that the road to the fulfillment that we hear so much about today lies in the valley. To begin with, the wife has to build her husband spiritually, physically, and emotionally, and make sure her home is intact so that Satan cannot enter. If the husband fails, it is the wife's fault, and if the marriage collapses, she will be held responsible. I am convinced that we can save our marriages. The bible says, "Love burns like blazing fire, like a mighty flame. Many waters cannot quench love; rivers cannot wash it away". (Songs of Solomon 8:6-7). Marriage is a divine concept. Let's be committed to the concept. Committed to each other, and, above all, committed to the Lord. Let's stand together and fight this disease that's killing our world silently. We deserve to be happy. We can make it work. I have done it, by putting life into my dead marriage through the power of God. Now I am the happiest woman. I just renewed my vows with a beautiful wedding. My hard-to-handle man is now a changed husband. My difficult man is now an easy man. He goes to church on time, reads the Bible, and prays with me every morning and night. He is a father, a husband, and a lover. I thank the Lord I stayed and did not follow my mind to break my family. I have my husband all to myself. My children are happier, we can all laugh together. I hope other women can take this approach, it's worth a try. Marriage under pressure is a challenge, a failed challenge is a broken life, and for every broken life, there is a second chance. Our God is a God of second chances.

Proud Husband!

THE POWER OF PRAYER AND FASTING

There is power in prayer and fasting that can do miracles in your marriage. Prayer is a way of communicating with our father in heaven, our maker.

Prayer is the practice of the presence of God. It is the place where hope is lifted and supplication is made and pride is abandoned. Prayer is where we present our request and claim dependence upon God. It is the needful practice of a Christian.

It gives us the privilege of touching the heart of the Father through the Son of God, Jesus Christ. Too often, we ignore prayer and seek to accomplish in the strength of our own will those things that we desire and wish to happen. In so doing, we have made God a second choice in our lives. That's why we don't see God's hand at work.

There is a vitality and power in prayer. When we come to God in prayer, we see his might and power. Prayer changes the one praying because in prayer, you are in the presence of God as you lay before him your complete self in confession and dependence. Also, prayer is a conversation with God, pouring out the soul before the

Lord. Seeking God and making supplications. It is intimacy with God and relating to God.

There is nothing to hide when, in quiet supplication, we are reaching into the deepest part of ourselves and admitting our needs and failures. By doing so, pride is stripped, our hearts are quieted, and we enjoy the presence of God (James 4:8).

The other benefit of prayer is finding peace (Philippians 4:6-7). Peace with God is what you receive from God through Jesus. There has to be peace between us and God before we can have peace with others. Our relationship has to be genuine. Peace inside of us is what enables us to withstand the storms of life. You need to have every confidence inside of you that with God, everything is possible. We live by external forces in the outside, so we have to trust in God, the everlasting Rock. Also, we cannot have peace until we have victory over our mind. Most of the things we worry about never happen. It is the devil who controls our mind. The mind is the greatest battlefield that Satan attacks. If you can, conquer your mind and clear it by thinking that divorce is not an answer for me because God says, "What God had joined together let no man put asunder." We should walk as a victor, not a loser. Don't quit and don't be anxious for anything. Live a peaceful life. We are God's children.

Prayer must be sincere, offered with reverence and godly fear, with a humble sense of our insignificance as creatures and of our own unworthiness as sinners, with earnest importance and with unhesitating submission to the divine will.

Prayer must be offered in faith that God exists, and is the hearer and answerer of prayer, and that he will fulfill his words. Ask, and ye shall receive.

Fasting means to abstain from certain food and/or drink for a specify period of time. Fasting is primarily a tool by which we humble ourselves before God, by subjugating the fleshes will to the spirit's will in reverence to God. The purpose of fasting is to clear the ground for greater spiritual breakthrough in our lives, and the lives of those we come into contact with. It is to loose the bands of wickedness, to undo the heavy burdens, and to let the oppressed go free, and that ye break every yoke. To resist the devil's temptation, and for spiritual power to cast out demons.

Prayer and fasting are the most powerful weapons of spiritual warfare that God has given to his children.

Prayer needs fasting for its full and perfect development. Prayer is the one hand with which we grasp the invisible; fasting is the other hand with which we let loose and cast away the visible. Also, fasting boosts the intensity and effectiveness of our prayer at least tenfold and hundredfold, which gives us victory in the midst of difficulty, the miraculous invading the possible and the supernatural intervention changing human intention.

Prayer and fasting are the weapons God has given us to fight Satan and his cohorts. It is up to us to pick up the weapons and learn how to use them. If we follow our tendency and wait for crisis to pick up our weapons, our lack of skill is likely to be exposed in defeat. Satan is a highly skilled adversary. His spiritual forces are experienced veterans, having waged war on mankind for thousands of years. They know our weaknesses and how best to exploit them. God calls to us to be good warriors, trained and skillful in using the weapons he has given us.

God will train those people who are willing to learn to fight.

David declared that God trained him to fight against the enemy and taught his hands to make war (Psalm 18:34). God also armed him with strength, agility, firm footing, strategic positioning, vision, and protection (Psalm 18:28-39). God will provide all of those things to us as well, yet we still are required to get up and fight through prayer and fasting.

I believe in the power of fasting as it relates to prayer. It is the atomic bomb that the Lord has given us to destroy the strongholds of evil.

As I said before, this is the strategy I used to overcome my trials. As I began to pray and fast, my confidence was in the Lord to help me. This is called "The Golden Key Prayer." All your focus is on the Lord your God, who is your only helper. Each day his presence encouraged me to continue. The longer I fasted and prayed, the more I sensed the presence of the Lord. The Holy Spirit refreshed my soul and spirit, and I experienced the joy of the Lord. My faith soared as I humbled myself and cried out to God and rejoiced in his presence. Things started working for me. I did ask my husband for us to go for counseling one time, and got other people involved in our business for a short period, then realized that it is a big mistake to involve other people or go for marriage counseling.

Remember that Satan knows how powerful prayer and fasting is, so he doesn't allow us to pray, he makes us weak. When we cannot pray, of course, we will not fast. But be strong and pray. If you can go on your knees and pray, you will experience the power of God. If families can pray, divorce won't be an answer. Moreover, if wives can pray fervently, every household will be intact and Satan will not enter into that house. There is nothing like the power of a praying woman or a praying wife. If only we can rise up to pray and fast, heaven will hear us and our situation can change. Don't settle for less. Consult God first before you go to marriage counselors. He who understands the power of prayer and fasting does not follow people or go for counseling. Don't war. God will turn your divorce into love if only you can believe in God.

There is no circumstance our God cannot change if we come to him in prayer. He hears our prayers. It doesn't matter what you have heard or been told, divorce is not an answer. Do not accept it or be afraid of anything; you have the power to change your situation.

There is a God who is mighty and powerful. The Bible says, "The king's heart is in the hand of the LORD, as the rivers of water: he turns it wherever He wishes." (Proverbs 21:1) You see he holds the heart of man, he can change it. There is a judge; his name is Master Jesus Christ. Do not limit God, he is bigger than DIVORCE.

FIGHT FOR YOUR MARRIAGE

Are you facing a storm in your marriage? Is your marriage on the rocks? Let Jesus calm your storm. He can restore your marriage.

First of all, you have to know that marriage has transitions. Marriage begins and ends, but in the middle falls love, anger, and dislike or hatred. These transitions are what you need to have knowledge about to have a long-lasting marriage. Marriage involves transitions, from the highs of the honeymoon, to the struggles of everyday life. And the biggest transition to be faced is when children enter the picture. So, it takes experience to recognize these shifts as normal.

Let's start with life. Life is complex. Most people try to define life. Life is how you make it. The more you put in, the more it becomes hopeless. Just like marriage, the more love you give, the less love you get in return. But all these answers can be found in the living word of God. Jesus is the answer to all these questions.

Jesus Christ is the embodiment of life. When you take the Lord from your life, you have no life. No Jesus, no life, is very simple. People are dreaming of a good life, but God is our life.

We are caught up in the misery of the knowledge of how life can be in a marriage. There are three transitions we have to pass through to be successful in marriage.

The first phrase is the beginning period. This is from the time couples meet and start dating until marriage and honeymoon. This is the happy time when the excitement takes place. Nothing can come between the two people. Life is good. This phase is not important, because it is easy. This phase doesn't mean you have successes, but things are better.

The third phase is the ending period, when you pass through the turmoils of life and success. This is where you don't sweat for anything. You enjoy life, where everything is glamorous. People identify you as somebody. This is where you are reaping what you have sowed. Playing golf in the morning, signing checks for payroll. You are in charge.

The second phase is our focus. This is what your marriage depends on. This is where the storm hits hard. You are passing through the storms of life. This is where you don't know what to expect or what to do. Locked up in the middle, what would you do when divorce is coming, or when you spouse says, "I don't love you any more"? This is where the Satan knows that you are a believer. He realizes that he cannot have your soul; he will, however, do everything to take away your Christian testimony, to rob you of your effectiveness. It's also here that Satan wants to take away solid Christian marriages, and rob the church of its ability to be a leader. This is when marriage becomes a challenge, and the fight for your marriage begins. Most importantly, this is where God speaks his words to us. If you can take God with you through your transition of marriage, success will hit you like a bomb.

This phase is very crucial because we start blaming each other for our failures, for the things we did not accomplish before getting married. The husband has lost his identity as the head, cannot function as a husband, and starts to regret getting married. The wife cannot submit any longer, sex becomes meaningless; no one has a taste for it any longer. If children are involved, they begin to get confused about what's going on in their family.

But in the midst of all this problem, God speaks to us. Stand firm, you are not alone. I was there once. Seek God; he will lead you through your transitions of marriage. If only you can walk, move, sing, and dance, you can win. Don't stop, do not seek divorce, it is not an answer.

In life, we have to be prepared for any change. Life is not always going to be good. We face seasons every day. Are we well-prepared? I never thought it could happen to me until I experienced it. I was not prepared at all. The one mistake we make is that we forget that we are living in a world full of troubles, and we are not ready. And sometimes, God in his own power lets us pass through these trials, so he alone can have the glory. So remember that no season is permanent, it is just for a period of time. But how prepared you are will determine how long you stay in the storm. Fight harder, don't let anybody stop you. Things will change. We should never take our eyes from our source of strength and protection. God is our rock and our shield. Our strength comes from a true and loving relationship with him. I prayed and fasted for his wisdom, truth, and protection for myself and my marriage.

Fighting for your marriage is not easy. It was the hardest thing I ever did in my whole life, because I was determined to win. I knew I could have never succeeded if I had followed the voice of Satan or misleading friends and been among people with bad characters. I had to locate myself and my vision. A successful person always sticks to her vision. Do not let people take you down. Some people think that they have to voice their opinion to you about divorce; some people judge, or are even jealous of a person getting a divorce. It is common. And also, divorce can be a common topic of gossip.

Never go for counseling, because God is the King of all Kings, he is the Prince of Peace. Seek him harmlessly, and he will see you through. Discover and recover the formula. There nine things that I discovered and recovered that helped me with my marriage. First, I used to come to bed too late when my husband was already sleeping. By the time I was done with getting myself ready for bed, he was already sleeping. Bad idea. Do not go to bed late while your partner is asleep. Second, don't stay on the telephone or computer all night or watch television while your spouse is in bed waiting for you to come. Third, Is talking to the opposite sex for a long time on the phone while your spouse is around. It makes him feel jealous and abandoned. He will not tell you that he is jealous, but he is. He will feel neglected. Four, Please don't raise your voice during an argument. In a moment of anger, don't raise your voice to your spouse. It makes him angry, and that induces a quarrel. Moreover, do not show your anger against your spouse in public.

When people are around, do not do it, keep it until you come home and talk about it. Fifth, don't discuss your marriage with other people. There are people who you don't want to know what is going on in your marriage; they help to destroy your marriage with their negativity. I call them home wreckers. Six, never use sex as a punishment in a marriage. Even if you argue or fight with your spouse, you cannot withhold sex. Legally, he or she owns you. Remember, sex kills anger. Respecting your spouse is very important. Seven, don't use bad words, especially when children are involved. Eight, don't rush your wife when she is dressing. Women have to look good when coming out in public; they love to compare themselves with other women. So, give her time to show her beauty. Please keep in mind that women are emotional beings. Nine don't assume your spouse is all right. Always ask questions. Assumptions can hider a good marriage. Touching your spouse frequently means a lot. Let your spouse know that you care and help your spouse when he or she is doing anything. Support your spouse to achieve his or her goals, it counts. Most importantly, thank your spouse from time to time. Don't take your spouse for granted. Appreciate everything he does, be grateful and be proud of your spouse. And commend him or her.

When you are confused, don't give in. There is a God who upholds your life. He is always found in the transitional period. He doesn't show up in happy times, but the midst of trouble. He promises not to leave us nor forsake us.

Life is not magic, you must pass through phases of life to become successful.

Without transitions in your marriage, you will fail. Fight for your godly testimony and your covenant marriage. Our fight is God's word, and it is our weapon.

Let's join hands together and fight together so we can stop the horrors of divorce. We can break the mode of transmission together. It is teamwork.

"Never doubt that a small group of thoughtful, committed people can change the world. Indeed, it is the only thing that ever has". (Margaret Mead)

DIVORCE IS NOT AN ANSWER

GOD HATES DIVORCE. So should we. It is not an answer to any problem. God was there when you made a vow to your spouse on your wedding day, "FOR BETTER OR FOR WORSE." What happened shortly after that? God knew the pain, tears, all the rejection, deceit, and disappointment that divorce brings along. It doesn't come alone, that's why he said divorce is not an answer. It is deadly. It doesn't solve problems, it doesn't provide you with a satisfying life, it doesn't bear a beautiful child in a family, and it doesn't put an end to anything, especially when children are involved. It only brings you problems, and makes the family look ugly.

God created man and woman, and told them to be fruitful and multiply upon the earth. This was the first foundation established on the earth, and it creates like everything else: by God. Originally, God intended for man and woman to increase in number and not decrease in number. When a family divorces, they are decreasing in number.

Resist it, it is torture. It creates new problems, regrets, blaming, depression, loneliness, remorse, and failure. It leads to destruction.

Do not depart (divorce) from your mate.

We must understand that life is not sweet as honey, but neither is it full of sour taste. It is a mixture of both, and it depends upon the individual. So, the decision to divorce or remain together to work things out is one of the most important decisions you will ever make. Too often, the fallout from divorce is more devastating than many people realize when contemplating the move. Sometimes married couples do sincerely believe that the divorcing party and the children involved would be better off if they got out of the marriage. This is not true. Most divorced couples can never be the same.

Divorce creates problems and pain that never existed, especially with children. They are the ones who suffer the most. The hurt, disappointment, and confusion never go away. They most of the time believe that they are the cause of the divorce; therefore, there is no optimum time to divorce when children are involved, regardless of their age at the time of their parents' divorce. Children lose a great deal. They lose their protection and security, and sometimes the other parent moves away. The family structure plays a very important role in the lives of children. The parents should work together as much as possible to prevent the damage divorce can do to the children.

When divorce comes, couples don't just divorce, families divorce. It is not just between husband and wife, it is the whole family that divorces. That's why divorce is not an answer. The family unit is a vital part of the stability of young children. Mothers and fathers are an important resource for their children. They give love, provide support, and teach skills and knowledge about life, as well as serve as a role model. To break this unit through divorce can be a heart-wrenching experience for the children — which means, we have failed the children God has entrusted to us to nurture and lead. And we will die a shameful death. If you loved you spouse to marry him or her, and have children, then don't you think it's worth trying to work out your differences? Most parents would wish for their children's lives nothing less than a valley of blessing and a pleasant life of peacefulness and joy, but when divorce comes, this dream is shattered.

Divorce is forever. It never goes away. Even though some people may say it is good in a destructive relationship, it is still not an answer. There are always going to be regrets and torment, and it remains a critical experience. Divorce is like losing a parent. When the other parent is dead and gone, it is final. But divorce also lasts forever. It leaves a deep hole that will never be filled, and always brings fresh memories despite the time of divorce.

Divorce is Satan's way of destroying our lives, homes, marriages, and most of all, our children. Please stand with me to put an end to the transmission of this terrible disease that has taken over this society today. One of marriage's most remarkable attributes is that it is a living entity. Full of near-death, followed by rebirth. Before you call it quits, get help from God. Do everything to save your marriage. It is important to find ways to avoid divorce, reunite your family, and minimize the effect of divorce that children go through.

Remember, there is no good divorce. No matter how good or bad it is, a divorce is a divorce. You still feel divided inside. It is not an answer. Through all the turmoil in the beginning, I can now stand and thank God. I am the happiest woman. I hear all the nice words from my husband every time: "I love you," "You are beautiful." I do not drive myself; he takes me everywhere I want to go. He compliments me for everything I do. Our love life is very good. Thanks to God, I did not chose divorce as an answer, but "till death do us part." Can you say the same thing today?

Love is patient, love is kind. It does not envy, it does not boast, it is not proud. It is not rude, it is not self-seeking, it is not easily angered, it keeps no record of wrongs. Love does not delight in evil but rejoices with the truth. It always protects, always trusts, always hopes, always perseveres. Love never fails. (1 Corinthians 13: 4-8)

He who finds a wife finds what is good and receives favor from the LORD. (Proverbs 18:22)

Above all, Love each other deeply, because love covers over a multitude of sin. (1 Peter 4:8)

Your wife will be like a fruitful vine within your house; your sons will be like olive shoots around your table. Thus is the man blessed who fears the LORD. (Psalm 128:3-4)

May the Lord make your love increase and overflow for each other. (Thessalonians 3:12)

May your fountain be blessed, and may you rejoice in the wife of your youth. May you ever be captivated by her love.

(Proverbs 5: 18-19)

A wife of noble character is her husband's crown.

(Proverbs 12: 4)

There is no fear in love. But perfect love drives out fear.

(1 John 4:18)

We know and rely on the love God has for us. God is love. Whoever lives in love lives in God, and God in him.

(1 John 4: 16)

ABOUT THE AUTHOR

Sia F. Dean was born in Kono district, Sierra Leone, West Africa, and moved to the United States when she was twenty-six years old. She was raised as a Muslim, and converted to Christianity shortly after arriving in the United States. Sia is the mother of seven children, and has been married to her husband, Charles S. Dean II, for fifteen years.

Divorce Is Not an Answer is the first book she has written.

Printed in the United States
105892LV00007B/358-450/P